BOOK 1

Retail Revolution:

The Ultimate Guide to Starting Your Wholesale and Retail Business

ISBN: 9798334199477

by- *Arya Gupta*

Year of publishing- 2024

Copyright © 2024

All rights reserved. No part of this book may be reproduced or transmitted in any form or by any means, electronic or mechanical, including photocopying, recording, or by any information storage and retrieval system, without the written permission of the publisher, except where permitted by law.

This is a work of non-fiction. Names, characters, places, and incidents either are products of the author's imagination or are used fictitiously. Any resemblance to actual events, locales, or persons, living or dead, is entirely coincidental.

Cover design by *Arya Gupta*

ISBN: 9798334199477

Published by Self-Published

For permissions or inquiries, contact: iaryaguptaa@example.com

First Edition, July 2024

Printed in the INDIA

Table Of Contents

Introduction 6
- Why Wholesale and Retail? 9
- Your Roadmap to Success 9
- Why This Guide? 10
- Let's Get Started 11

Chapter 1: Business Planning 12
    1.1 Defining Your Vision, Mission, and Goals 13
    1.2 Conducting Market Research 14
    1.3 Crafting a Unique Value Proposition 15
    1.4 Developing a Business Model 16
    1.5 Legal and Regulatory Considerations 17
    1.6 Financial Planning 18
    1.7 Building a Strong Brand 19
    1.8 Marketing and Sales Strategy 20
    1.9 Risk Management 21
    1.10 Execution Plan 21

Chapter 2: Sourcing Products 24
- Introduction to Product Sourcing 24
- Understanding Your Market 24

- Finding Reliable Suppliers 25
- Evaluating Suppliers 26
- Negotiating with Suppliers 28
- Managing Your Inventory 29
- Building Strong Supplier Relationships 31
  o Conclusion 32

Chapter 3: Marketing Strategies 34
- Introduction to Marketing 34
- Understanding Your Target Market 34
- Building Your Brand 35
- Digital Marketing Strategies 36
- Traditional Marketing Strategies 40
- Customer Engagement and Retention 41
- Measuring and Analyzing Marketing Efforts 42
  o Conclusion 44

Chapter 4: Managing Finances 45
- The Importance of Financial Management 46
- Creating a Budget 46
- Pricing Strategies 48
- Managing Cash Flow 49

- Funding Options 50
- Financial Tools and Resources 52
- Building a Financial Team 53
  o Conclusion 53

Case Studies/Examples 55

Case Study 1: The Rise of Eco-Goods Mart 55

Case Study 2: TechZone's Wholesale Success 57

Case Study 3: Boutique Bliss Goes Online 59

Case Study 4: Gourmet Delights Wholesale Expansion 61

Case Study 5: Fitness Hub's Niche Market Strategy 63

Case Study 6: Artisan Craft Collective's Community Focus .. 65

Case Study 7: Pet Paradise's Customer-Centric Approach 67

Case Study 8: Trendy Threads' Social Media Success 69

Case Study 9: Green Grocers' Sustainable Growth 71

  o Conclusion 72

Preface

In the dynamic and ever-evolving world of commerce, the journey from a dream to a thriving wholesale and retail business can seem both exhilarating and daunting. As someone who has traversed this path, I understand the myriad of challenges and triumphs that await aspiring entrepreneurs. It is this journey that inspired me to write "Retail Revolution: The Ultimate Guide to Starting Your Wholesale and Retail Business."

This book is not merely a compilation of strategies and techniques; it is a comprehensive guide forged from real-world experiences, diligent research, and a deep passion for the retail industry. Whether you are a budding entrepreneur seeking to carve out your niche or a seasoned business owner looking to expand your horizons, this guide aims to provide you with valuable insights and practical tools to succeed.

Over the years, I have witnessed the transformative power of knowledge and the impact it can have on one's entrepreneurial journey. I have had the privilege of mentoring many individuals and helping them navigate the complexities of starting and growing their businesses. Through these experiences, I have distilled the essence of what it takes to thrive in the wholesale and retail sectors into this guide.

"Retail Revolution" is structured to take you step-by-step through the critical stages of establishing and scaling a business. From understanding the fundamental principles of wholesale and retail to mastering the art of market research, financial management, and customer engagement, each chapter is designed to equip you with the necessary skills and knowledge to achieve your business goals.

This book also delves into the practical aspects of running a business, offering actionable advice on sourcing products, managing operations, and leveraging marketing strategies to drive sales. Additionally, it addresses the inevitable challenges that come with entrepreneurship, providing strategies for overcoming obstacles and maintaining resilience.

As you embark on this journey, I encourage you to approach each chapter with an open mind and a willingness to learn. The path to success is rarely linear, but with determination, perseverance, and the right guidance, you can navigate the twists and turns with confidence.

I am deeply grateful for the support and encouragement of my family, friends, and mentors, without whom this book would not have been possible. It is my hope that "Retail Revolution" will serve as a valuable companion on your entrepreneurial journey, inspiring you to achieve new heights and revolutionize the world of retail.

Thank you for allowing me to be a part of your journey. Here's to your success and the exciting adventures that lie ahead.

Warm regards,

Arya Gupta

Introduction

- **Welcome to Your Retail Revolution**

Starting a wholesale and retail business is like embarking on a thrilling adventure. It's a journey filled with opportunities, challenges, and the potential for immense satisfaction. Whether you're dreaming of opening a trendy boutique, a bustling online store, or a comprehensive wholesale operation, this guide is designed to be your compass.

In the pages that follow, we'll walk you through every step of the process, from the initial spark of an idea to the grand opening and beyond. You'll learn the essentials of business planning, product sourcing, marketing strategies, and financial management, all tailored to help you build a thriving enterprise.

- **The Retail Landscape Today**

The retail industry has undergone a dramatic transformation in recent years. With the rise of e-commerce, the lines between physical and digital shopping have blurred, creating a dynamic marketplace. Consumers today are more informed, more connected, and have higher expectations than ever before.

This evolution presents both challenges and opportunities. On one hand, competition is fierce, and standing out requires innovation and strategic thinking. On the other hand, the digital revolution has lowered barriers to entry, making it possible for anyone with a passion and a plan to start their own retail business.

- **Why Wholesale and Retail?**

Combining wholesale and retail operations can offer significant advantages. Wholesale allows you to sell products in bulk to other retailers or businesses, providing a steady stream of revenue and expanding your market reach. Retail, whether online or in a brick-and-mortar store, allows you to connect directly with consumers, build brand loyalty, and command higher profit margins.

This dual approach can create a resilient business model, balancing the stability of wholesale with the growth potential of retail. By diversifying your revenue streams, you can better navigate market fluctuations and scale your business more effectively.

- **Your Roadmap to Success**

This guide is structured to take you step-by-step through the process of starting your wholesale and retail business. Here's a brief overview of what you can expect:

1. **Business Planning**: We'll start with the foundations, helping you to develop a solid business plan. This includes defining your vision, mission, and goals, conducting market research, and understanding your target audience.
2. **Sourcing Products**: Next, we'll delve into the world of product sourcing. You'll learn how to find reliable suppliers, negotiate deals, and manage inventory efficiently.
3. **Marketing Strategies**: Marketing is the lifeblood of any business. We'll explore both traditional and digital marketing techniques, from branding and social media to email marketing and SEO.
4. **Financial Management**: A strong financial foundation is crucial for long-term success. We'll cover budgeting, pricing strategies, cash flow management, and funding options.
5. **Operations and Growth**: Finally, we'll discuss the day-to-day operations of running your business and strategies for growth. This includes everything from customer service and logistics to scaling your business and exploring new markets.

- **Why This Guide?**

There are countless resources available on starting a business, but this guide is different. It's designed specifically for aspiring wholesale and retail entrepreneurs, with practical advice and real-world examples. Every chapter is packed with actionable insights, checklists, and templates to help you turn your dream into reality.

Moreover, this guide is written by someone who's been in your shoes. I understand the excitement, the doubts, and the determination that comes with starting a new venture. My goal is to share my knowledge and experiences to help you avoid common pitfalls and achieve your goals faster.

- **Let's Get Started**

The journey you're about to embark on will be challenging, but it will also be incredibly rewarding. As you read through this guide, remember that every successful business started with a single step. Take your time, stay focused, and don't be afraid to ask for help along the way.

Are you ready to start your retail revolution? Let's dive in and turn your vision into a thriving business!

Chapter 1: Business Planning

☩ The Blueprint of Your Business

Starting a wholesale and retail business without a plan is like setting sail without a map. Business planning is the foundation upon which your enterprise will stand, guiding your decisions, attracting investors, and setting you up for success. In this chapter, we'll create a comprehensive blueprint to navigate your business journey.

1.1 Defining Your Vision, Mission, and Goals

➢ Vision Statement

Your vision statement is a forward-looking declaration of your business's purpose and aspirations. It should inspire and guide your team and stakeholders, reflecting your long-term goals.

Example: "To be the leading provider of eco-friendly home goods, enriching lives with sustainable products that blend quality and affordability."

➢ Mission Statement

Your mission statement outlines the fundamental purpose of your business, describing what you do, for whom, and how. It should be concise and clear, capturing the essence of your operations.

Example: "*We offer high-quality, eco-friendly home goods that promote sustainability and enhance daily living, ensuring customer satisfaction through innovation and exceptional service.*"

> ➢ **Setting SMART Goals**

Goals provide direction and benchmarks for your business. Ensure they are Specific, Measurable, Achievable, Relevant, and Time-bound (SMART).

Example: "*Increase online sales by 20% in the next six months through targeted social media campaigns and improved user experience.*"

1.2 Conducting Market Research

> ➢ **Understanding Your Market**

Market research involves gathering, analyzing, and interpreting information about your target market, competitors, and industry. This data helps you make informed decisions and identify opportunities and threats.

> ➢ **Identifying Your Target Audience**

Define your ideal customers based on demographics, psychographics, and behavior. Create detailed buyer personas to understand their needs, preferences, and purchasing habits.

Example: "*Our target audience consists of eco-conscious consumers aged 25-45, primarily urban dwellers with a moderate to high income, interested in sustainable living.*"

> ➤ **Analyzing Competitors**

Identify your direct and indirect competitors. Analyze their strengths, weaknesses, pricing, marketing strategies, and customer feedback. This will help you position your business and identify gaps in the market.

> ➤ **Assessing Market Trends**

Stay informed about industry trends, consumer behavior, and technological advancements. Use sources like industry reports, news articles, and market research firms to gather insights.

1.3 Crafting a Unique Value Proposition

> ➤ **What Makes You Stand Out?**

Your unique value proposition (UVP) is a clear statement that explains how your product solves a problem, the specific benefits it delivers, and why customers should choose you over competitors.

Example: "Our eco-friendly home goods combine sustainability with stylish design, offering customers a guilt-free way to enhance their living spaces without compromising on quality."

➤ **Communicating Your UVP**

Ensure your UVP is prominently featured in all your marketing materials, including your website, social media profiles, and advertising campaigns. It should resonate with your target audience and clearly convey the unique benefits you offer.

1.4 Developing a Business Model

➤ **Choosing the Right Business Model**

Your business model defines how your company creates, delivers, and captures value. Common models in wholesale and retail include direct-to-consumer, subscription-based, and B2B sales.

Example: "We will operate a direct-to-consumer model, selling our products through an online store and partnering with select retail outlets for wider distribution."

> ### Revenue Streams

Identify all potential revenue streams, including product sales, subscription fees, affiliate marketing, and more. Diversifying your income sources can enhance financial stability.

> ### Cost Structure

Outline your fixed and variable costs, including production, marketing, staffing, and operational expenses. Understanding your cost structure helps in pricing your products and managing cash flow.

1.5 Legal and Regulatory Considerations

> ### Business Structure

Choose the appropriate legal structure for your business, such as sole proprietorship, partnership, LLC, or corporation. Each structure has different implications for liability, taxes, and regulatory requirements.

> ### Registering Your Business

Register your business name and obtain any necessary licenses and permits. This varies by location and industry, so consult local regulations and seek legal advice if needed.

> ### Intellectual Property

Protect your brand with trademarks, copyrights, and patents as applicable. This safeguards your intellectual property and ensures you have the legal right to use your business name, logo, and product designs.

> ### Compliance

Ensure compliance with industry-specific regulations, including health and safety standards, environmental laws, and labor laws. Staying compliant helps avoid legal issues and builds trust with customers and stakeholders.

1.6 Financial Planning

> ### Initial Investment

Estimate the initial investment required to start your business. This includes costs for inventory, equipment, marketing, legal fees, and working capital. Create a detailed budget to plan your expenditures.

> **Pricing Strategy**

Develop a pricing strategy that covers your costs and achieves your desired profit margin while remaining competitive. Consider factors like production costs, market demand, and competitor pricing.

> **Financial Projections**

Prepare financial projections for at least the first three years, including income statements, cash flow statements, and balance sheets. These projections help you understand your business's financial viability and attract investors.

> **Funding Options**

Explore various funding options, such as personal savings, loans, grants, and investor funding. Each option has its pros and cons, so choose the one that best fits your needs and business goals.

1.7 Building a Strong Brand

> **Brand Identity**

Your brand identity includes your business name, logo, colors, typography, and overall visual style. It should reflect your values, mission, and the personality of your brand.

> Brand Story

Craft a compelling brand story that connects with your audience on an emotional level. Share the inspiration behind your business, your journey, and what sets you apart from competitors.

> Brand Consistency

Ensure consistency across all touchpoints, including your website, social media, packaging, and customer service. Consistent branding builds recognition and trust with your audience.

1.8 Marketing and Sales Strategy

> Marketing Plan

Develop a comprehensive marketing plan outlining your strategies for reaching and engaging your target audience. Include tactics for digital marketing, content marketing, social media, email marketing, and more.

> Sales Strategy

Define your sales strategy, including your sales channels, sales team structure, and sales tactics. Consider both online and offline sales channels to maximize your reach.

> Customer Relationship Management (CRM)

Implement a CRM system to manage customer interactions and data. This helps you build strong relationships, improve customer satisfaction, and increase retention.

1.9 Risk Management

> Identifying Risks

Identify potential risks that could impact your business, such as market fluctuations, supply chain disruptions, or regulatory changes. Assess the likelihood and impact of each risk.

> Mitigation Strategies

Develop strategies to mitigate identified risks. This could include diversifying suppliers, creating contingency plans, or purchasing insurance.

> Monitoring and Review

Regularly monitor your risk management strategies and review their effectiveness. Be prepared to adjust your plans as necessary to adapt to changing circumstances.

1.10 Execution Plan

➤ **Milestones and Timelines**

Set clear milestones and timelines for key tasks and goals. This helps you stay on track and measure progress.

➤ **Accountability**

Assign responsibilities to team members and hold them accountable for their tasks. Clear communication and regular check-ins are crucial for successful execution.

➤ **Continuous Improvement**

Adopt a mindset of continuous improvement. Regularly review your business plan, seek feedback, and be willing to make changes to enhance your business's performance.

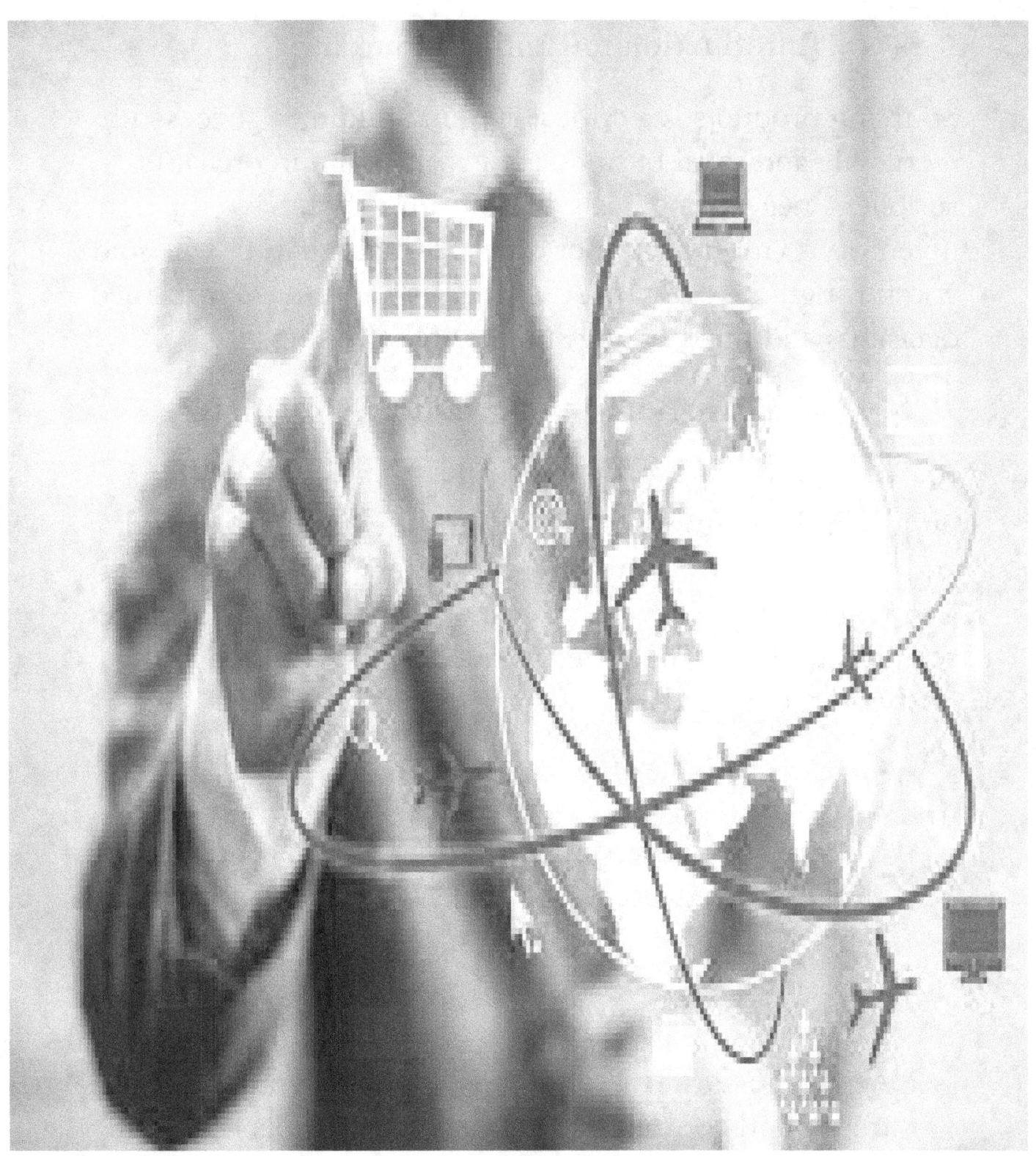

Chapter 2: Sourcing Products

✦ Introduction to Product Sourcing

Sourcing products is a critical step in building a successful wholesale and retail business. It involves finding reliable suppliers, negotiating deals, and ensuring you have the right inventory to meet customer demand. This chapter will guide you through the entire process, helping you make informed decisions and build strong supplier relationships.

✦ Understanding Your Market

Before you start sourcing products, it's essential to understand your market. This means identifying the needs and preferences of your target customers, analyzing trends, and evaluating your competitors. Conduct thorough market research to determine what products are in demand and how you can differentiate your offerings.

> Steps to Understanding Your Market:

1. **Identify Your Target Audience**: Define who your ideal customers are. Consider demographics, buying behavior, and preferences.

2. **Analyze Market Trends**: Stay updated with industry trends and consumer preferences. Use tools like Google Trends and industry reports.

3. **Evaluate Competitors**: Study your competitors to understand their product range, pricing strategies, and market positioning.

✦ Finding Reliable Suppliers

The success of your business heavily relies on the quality and reliability of your suppliers. Here are some steps to find the best suppliers for your wholesale and retail business:

➤ Types of Suppliers:

1. **Manufacturers**: Directly source from manufacturers to get the best prices and control over product quality.

2. **Distributors/Wholesalers**: These intermediaries buy in bulk from manufacturers and sell to retailers. They offer a wide range of products but may come with higher prices.

3. **Dropshippers**: Dropshipping allows you to sell products without holding inventory. The supplier ships products directly to customers on your behalf.

➢ **How to Find Suppliers:**

1. **Online Marketplaces**: Platforms like Alibaba, Global Sources, and Made-in-China are excellent for finding manufacturers and wholesalers.

2. **Trade Shows**: Attend industry trade shows to meet suppliers, see products firsthand, and establish relationships.

3. **Industry Associations**: Join industry associations to access directories and resources for finding reputable suppliers.

4. **Referrals**: Ask for recommendations from industry peers and network with other business owners.

✦ **Evaluating Suppliers**

Once you've identified potential suppliers, it's crucial to evaluate them thoroughly to ensure they meet your standards. Here's how to assess suppliers effectively:

➤ Criteria for Evaluation:

1. **Product Quality**: Request samples to evaluate the quality of products. Check for consistency and compliance with industry standards.

2. **Pricing**: Compare prices from multiple suppliers. Ensure the pricing aligns with your budget and allows for a reasonable profit margin.

3. **Reliability**: Research the supplier's track record. Look for reviews, testimonials, and any history of disputes.

4. **Communication**: Effective communication is key. Ensure the supplier is responsive and transparent in their dealings.

5. **Capacity**: Ensure the supplier can handle your order volume and deliver products within your required timeframe.

➤ Questions to Ask Potential Suppliers:

1. **What are your payment terms and conditions?**

2. What is your minimum order quantity (MOQ)?
3. Do you offer any discounts for bulk orders?
4. Can you provide references from other clients?
5. What is your return and refund policy?

✦ Negotiating with Suppliers

Negotiation is an art that can significantly impact your bottom line. Here are some tips to help you negotiate effectively with suppliers:

> **Negotiation Tips:**

1. **Be Prepared**: Do your homework and understand the market rates for the products you're sourcing.

2. **Build Relationships**: Establish a good rapport with your suppliers. Long-term relationships often lead to better deals.

3. **Be Clear About Your Needs**: Clearly communicate your requirements, including quality standards, delivery times, and payment terms.

4. **Ask for Discounts**: Don't hesitate to ask for discounts, especially for bulk orders or long-term contracts.

5. **Consider Total Cost**: Look beyond the unit price. Consider shipping costs, import duties, and other expenses.

➢ Common Negotiation Tactics:

1. **Bundling Orders**: Combine multiple orders to negotiate better prices.

2. **Extended Contracts**: Offer a long-term contract in exchange for better pricing or terms.

3. **Payment Terms**: Negotiate favorable payment terms, such as longer credit periods or partial payments.

✣ Managing Your Inventory

Effective inventory management ensures you have the right products available when your customers need them. Here are some strategies for managing your inventory efficiently:

> Inventory Management Techniques:

1. **Just-in-Time (JIT)**: Order inventory only when needed to reduce holding costs. This requires reliable suppliers and efficient logistics.

2. **ABC Analysis**: Categorize inventory into three groups (A, B, C) based on importance and value. Focus on managing 'A' items closely.

3. **Safety Stock**: Maintain a buffer stock to handle unexpected demand spikes or supply chain disruptions.

4. **Regular Audits**: Conduct regular inventory audits to ensure accuracy and identify discrepancies.

> Tools for Inventory Management:

1. **Inventory Management Software**: Use tools like TradeGecko, Zoho Inventory, or QuickBooks to track inventory levels, sales, and orders.

2. **Barcoding Systems**: Implement barcoding to streamline inventory tracking and reduce errors.

3. **Demand Forecasting**: Use historical sales data and market trends to predict future demand and adjust inventory levels accordingly.

✚ Building Strong Supplier Relationships

Strong relationships with your suppliers can lead to better deals, priority service, and long-term success. Here's how to build and maintain these relationships:

> Tips for Building Relationships:

1. **Communicate Regularly**: Maintain open and honest communication with your suppliers. Keep them informed about your business needs and any changes.

2. **Pay on Time**: Honor payment terms to build trust and credibility.

3. **Provide Feedback**: Offer constructive feedback on product quality and service. This helps suppliers improve and shows you value their partnership.

4. **Collaborate on Promotions**: Work with suppliers on joint promotions or marketing campaigns to boost sales for both parties.

5. **Be Loyal**: Loyalty can lead to preferential treatment and better terms. Avoid frequently switching suppliers without valid reasons.

o Conclusion

Sourcing products is a foundational aspect of your wholesale and retail business. By understanding your market, finding reliable suppliers, evaluating them carefully, negotiating effectively, managing your inventory, and building strong relationships, you can ensure a steady supply of high-quality products that meet your customers' needs.

Remember, successful product sourcing is not just about finding the cheapest supplier; it's about building a network of reliable partners who can support your business growth. As you move forward, use the insights and strategies outlined in this chapter to create a robust sourcing plan that sets the stage for your retail revolution.

Chapter 3: Marketing Strategies

✥ Introduction to Marketing

Marketing is the bridge between your products and your customers. It's how you communicate your value, build relationships, and drive sales. In this chapter, we'll explore various marketing strategies to help you reach your target audience, create a strong brand, and grow your business. From digital tactics to traditional methods, you'll learn how to craft a comprehensive marketing plan that aligns with your business goals.

✥ Understanding Your Target Market

➤ Identifying Your Audience

Your marketing efforts will only be effective if you understand who you are trying to reach. Define your ideal customer using:

- **Demographics**: Age, gender, income, education level, and occupation.
- **Psychographics**: Interests, hobbies, values, and lifestyle.
- **Behavioral Traits**: Shopping habits, brand loyalty, and purchasing behaviors.

Create detailed customer personas to visualize your target market. These personas should include names, backgrounds, and motivations to help you better understand and communicate with your audience.

➢ Market Research

Conducting thorough market research is crucial for understanding your industry, competitors, and potential customers. Methods include:

- **Surveys and Questionnaires**: Gather direct feedback from potential customers.
- **Focus Groups**: Conduct group discussions to dive deeper into customer opinions.
- **Interviews**: Have one-on-one conversations for in-depth insights.

Analyze your competitors to identify market gaps and opportunities. Look at their strengths and weaknesses, customer reviews, and marketing strategies to learn what works and what doesn't.

✚ Building Your Brand

➢ Brand Identity

Your brand identity is what sets you apart from the competition. Develop:

- **A Unique Brand Name**: Choose a name that's memorable, easy to pronounce, and reflects your business.
- **A Distinctive Logo**: Design a logo that represents your brand visually. Hire a professional designer if necessary.
- **A Tagline**: Create a catchy and meaningful tagline that captures the essence of your business.

➢ Brand Voice and Messaging

Establish a consistent tone and style for all communications. Whether you're writing social media posts, emails, or website content, your brand voice should be recognizable. Craft a compelling brand story that resonates with your audience, highlighting your mission, values, and what makes you unique.

✦ Digital Marketing Strategies

➢ Social Media Marketing

Social media platforms are powerful tools for reaching and engaging with your audience. Here's how to maximize your impact:

- **Platform Selection**: Choose platforms where your target audience is most active. Popular options include Facebook, Instagram, Twitter, LinkedIn, and TikTok.
- **Content Calendar:** Plan and schedule your posts in advance. Include a mix of promotional content, educational posts, and engaging visuals.
- **Engagement**: Interact with your followers by responding to comments, messages, and mentions. Host contests, Q&A sessions, and live streams to boost engagement.
- **Paid Advertising**: Use social media ads to increase your reach. Target specific demographics and interests to attract potential customers.

➢ Content Marketing

Content marketing helps you attract and retain customers by providing valuable information. Key tactics include:

- **Blogging**: Start a blog on your website to share industry insights, how-to guides, and product updates. Optimize your posts with SEO techniques to improve search engine rankings.
- **SEO (Search Engine Optimization)**: Use keyword research to identify terms your audience is searching for. Incorporate these keywords into your website content, meta descriptions, and blog posts.
- **Multimedia Content**: Diversify your content with videos, infographics, and podcasts. Create tutorials,

product demos, and behind-the-scenes videos to engage your audience.

➢ Email Marketing

Email marketing remains one of the most effective channels for reaching your customers. Here's how to leverage it:

- **Building an Email List**: Use lead magnets like free eBooks, discounts, or exclusive content to encourage sign-ups. Ensure your opt-in forms are prominently displayed on your website.

- **Segmentation**: Divide your email list into segments based on customer behavior, demographics, and purchase history. This allows you to send personalized and relevant content.

- **Effective Campaigns**: Design email campaigns with compelling subject lines, clear calls to action, and visually appealing templates. Track open rates, click-through rates, and conversions to measure success.

➢ Influencer Marketing

Partnering with influencers can amplify your brand message. Steps to effective influencer marketing include:

- **Identifying Influencers**: Look for influencers who align with your brand values and have a following that matches your target audience.

- **Collaborations**: Work with influencers on product reviews, unboxing videos, sponsored posts, and giveaways. Provide them with clear guidelines and creative freedom.

- **Measuring Success**: Track the performance of influencer campaigns through engagement metrics, referral traffic, and sales conversions. Adjust your strategy based on results.

✠ Traditional Marketing Strategies

➢ Print Advertising

Despite the digital shift, print advertising still holds value. Here's how to utilize it effectively:

- **Brochures and Flyers**: Distribute these at local events, trade shows, and in-store. Ensure they are visually appealing and convey key information.
- **Magazines and Newspapers**: Advertise in publications that your target audience reads. This can enhance your credibility and reach.

➢ Events and Trade Shows

Participating in events and trade shows provides opportunities to network and showcase your products:

- **Trade Shows**: Book a booth at industry trade shows to connect with potential buyers and partners. Prepare engaging presentations and promotional materials.
- **In-Store Events**: Host events like product launches, workshops, and exclusive sales. Promote these events through social media and email marketing to drive attendance.

> Direct Mail

Direct mail can be a personal and effective way to reach customers:

- **Targeted Mailers**: Send personalized postcards, catalogs, or brochures to specific segments of your audience. Highlight special offers or new products.
- **Incentives**: Include coupons or discount codes to encourage immediate action.

Customer Engagement and Retention

> Customer Service

Exceptional customer service is key to building loyalty:

- **Responsiveness**: Address customer inquiries and issues promptly and professionally. Use multiple channels such as phone, email, and social media.
- **Personalization**: Personalize interactions by addressing customers by name and referencing their purchase history.

> Loyalty Programs

Rewarding repeat customers helps retain them:

- **Loyalty Rewards**: Offer points for purchases, referrals, and social media engagement. Customers can redeem points for discounts or free products.
- **Exclusive Access**: Provide loyalty program members with early access to new products, special promotions, and exclusive events.

➢ Community Building

Creating a sense of community fosters brand loyalty:

- **Social Media Groups**: Start and actively manage Facebook or LinkedIn groups where customers can share experiences, ask questions, and connect.
- **User-Generated Content**: Encourage customers to share photos, reviews, and stories related to your products. Feature this content on your social media and website.
-

✦ **Measuring and Analyzing Marketing Efforts**

➢ Key Performance Indicators (KPIs)

Tracking KPIs helps you measure the success of your marketing strategies:

- **Website Traffic**: Use tools like Google Analytics to monitor the number of visitors, page views, and user behavior on your website.
- **Conversion Rates**: Track the percentage of visitors who take a desired action, such as making a purchase or signing up for your newsletter.
- **Customer Acquisition Cost (CAC)**: Calculate the cost of acquiring a new customer by dividing total marketing expenses by the number of new customers.
- **Customer Lifetime Value (CLTV)**: Estimate the total revenue a customer will generate over their lifetime with your business.

> ➤ Adjusting Strategies

Regularly reviewing and adjusting your marketing strategies is crucial:

- **Analyze Data**: Use analytics tools to gather data and gain insights into the performance of different marketing channels and campaigns.
- **Refine Tactics**: Identify what's working and what's not. Adjust your strategies accordingly to improve effectiveness and ROI.
- **Stay Adaptable**: Be prepared to pivot and try new approaches based on changing market conditions and customer preferences.

- **Conclusion**

Marketing is an ongoing process that requires creativity, consistency, and a deep understanding of your customers. By leveraging both digital and traditional marketing strategies, you can build a strong brand, connect with your audience, and drive sustainable growth for your wholesale and retail business. Remember, the key to successful marketing is to stay adaptable, listen to your customers, and always be ready to innovate.

Chapter 4: Managing Finances

✢ The Importance of Financial Management

Effective financial management is the cornerstone of any successful business. For wholesale and retail entrepreneurs, understanding your finances goes beyond simply balancing the books. It's about making informed decisions that drive growth, ensuring sustainability, and preparing for unexpected challenges.

In this chapter, we'll cover the essential components of financial management, including budgeting, pricing strategies, cash flow management, and funding options. By the end, you'll have the tools and knowledge to take control of your business finances and steer your company toward long-term success.

✢ Creating a Budget

➢ The Foundation of Financial Planning

A budget is a financial roadmap for your business. It helps you allocate resources, plan for expenses, and set revenue targets. Here's a step-by-step guide to creating an effective budget:

1. **List Your Income Sources**: Identify all potential income sources, including sales revenue, loans, and investments. Estimate your monthly and annual income based on market research and historical data.

2. **Identify Fixed and Variable Costs**: Fixed costs remain constant regardless of your sales volume (e.g., rent, salaries). Variable costs fluctuate with your business activity (e.g., inventory, shipping). List and categorize your expenses accordingly.
3. **Forecast Sales and Expenses**: Use historical data and market trends to forecast your sales and expenses. Be conservative with your estimates to avoid overestimating your revenue.
4. **Set Financial Goals**: Define clear financial goals for your business. These might include revenue targets, profit margins, or cost reduction objectives. Ensure your budget aligns with these goals.
5. **Monitor and Adjust**: Regularly review your budget and compare it with actual performance. Adjust your budget as needed to reflect changes in your business environment or strategy.

> Budgeting Tools and Software

Utilizing budgeting tools and software can simplify the budgeting process and provide valuable insights. Some popular options include:

- **QuickBooks**: Comprehensive accounting software that offers budgeting, expense tracking, and financial reporting.
- **Excel**: A flexible tool for creating customized budgets and financial models.

- **Wave**: Free accounting software suitable for small businesses, offering basic budgeting features.

Pricing Strategies

> Finding the Right Balance

Setting the right prices for your products is crucial for profitability and competitiveness. Here are some pricing strategies to consider:

1. **Cost-Plus Pricing**: Calculate your total costs (production, overhead, etc.) and add a markup to ensure a profit. This method ensures you cover your costs but might not be competitive.
2. **Competitive Pricing**: Set your prices based on competitor analysis. This approach helps you remain competitive but requires constant market monitoring.
3. **Value-Based Pricing**: Set prices based on the perceived value of your products to the customer. This strategy can justify higher prices if you offer unique benefits or superior quality.
4. **Discount Pricing**: Offer discounts to attract customers and increase sales volume. Use this strategy carefully to avoid eroding your profit margins.
5. **Dynamic Pricing**: Adjust prices based on demand, market conditions, or customer segments. This approach maximizes revenue but requires sophisticated data analysis.

> Implementing Your Pricing Strategy

1. **Analyze Costs and Margins**: Understand your costs and set prices that provide a healthy profit margin. Factor in all costs, including production, shipping, and marketing.
2. **Understand Your Market**: Research your target market and competitors. Know what your customers are willing to pay and how your prices compare to competitors.
3. **Test and Adjust**: Start with a pricing strategy and monitor its impact on sales and profitability. Be prepared to adjust your prices based on feedback and market changes.
4. **Communicate Value**: Ensure your customers understand the value they receive for the price. Highlight unique features, benefits, and quality to justify your pricing.

✦ **Managing Cash Flow**

> Keeping Your Business Liquid

Cash flow is the lifeblood of your business. Positive cash flow ensures you have the funds to cover expenses, invest in growth, and navigate financial challenges. Here's how to manage your cash flow effectively:

1. **Monitor Cash Flow Regularly**: Use cash flow statements to track your income and expenses. Regular

monitoring helps you identify trends and potential issues.
2. **Optimize Inventory Management**: Avoid overstocking or understocking by managing your inventory efficiently. Overstocking ties up cash, while understocking can lead to lost sales.
3. **Manage Receivables and Payables**: Implement efficient invoicing and collection processes to ensure timely payments from customers. Negotiate favorable payment terms with suppliers to manage cash outflows.
4. **Maintain a Cash Reserve**: Set aside a portion of your profits as a cash reserve for emergencies or unexpected expenses. This provides a financial cushion and peace of mind.
5. **Control Operating Expenses**: Regularly review your operating expenses and identify areas for cost reduction. This might include renegotiating contracts, reducing waste, or streamlining operations.

✚ Funding Options

➤ Financing Your Business

Securing the right funding is crucial for starting and growing your wholesale and retail business. Here are some common funding options:

1. **Self-Funding**: Using personal savings or assets to fund your business. This option involves less risk but may limit your financial resources.

2. **Bank Loans**: Traditional loans from banks or financial institutions. These typically require a solid business plan and collateral but offer larger sums of capital.
3. **Small Business Grants**: Government or private grants available for specific industries or business types. These do not require repayment but are often competitive.
4. **Venture Capital**: Investment from venture capitalists in exchange for equity in your business. This option provides significant capital but involves giving up some control.
5. **Crowdfunding**: Raising small amounts of money from a large number of people, typically via online platforms. This can also serve as a marketing tool to build a customer base.
6. **Angel Investors**: Wealthy individuals who invest in startups in exchange for equity or convertible debt. They often provide mentorship and networking opportunities in addition to funding.

➢ Choosing the Right Option

When selecting a funding option, consider the following factors:

1. **Business Stage**: Early-stage businesses might rely more on self-funding, grants, or angel investors, while established businesses might seek bank loans or venture capital.

2. **Funding Needs**: Determine how much capital you need and match it with the appropriate funding source. Smaller amounts might be raised through crowdfunding, while larger sums might require venture capital or bank loans.
3. **Risk Tolerance**: Assess your willingness to take on debt or give up equity. Choose a funding option that aligns with your risk tolerance and long-term goals.
4. **Repayment Terms**: Understand the repayment terms and conditions of any loan or investment. Ensure you can meet the obligations without compromising your business operations.

✛ Financial Tools and Resources

➢ Leveraging Technology

Utilizing financial tools and resources can streamline your financial management and provide valuable insights. Here are some recommended tools:

1. **Accounting Software**: QuickBooks, Xero, or FreshBooks for comprehensive accounting and financial reporting.
2. **Budgeting Apps**: YNAB (You Need a Budget) or Mint for personal and business budgeting.
3. **Cash Flow Management**: Float or Pulse for monitoring and forecasting cash flow.

4. **Expense Tracking**: Expensify or Receipt Bank for tracking and managing expenses.
5. **Financial Planning**: LivePlan or PlanGuru for business planning and financial forecasting.

✠ Building a Financial Team

➢ When to Seek Professional Help

As your business grows, managing finances becomes more complex. Building a financial team can provide the expertise and support you need. Consider hiring or consulting with:

1. **Accountants**: For bookkeeping, tax preparation, and financial advice.
2. **Financial Advisors**: For strategic financial planning and investment advice.
3. **CFOs (Chief Financial Officers)**: For overseeing financial operations and providing high-level financial strategy.

o Conclusion

Effective financial management is essential for the success and sustainability of your wholesale and retail business. By creating a solid budget, implementing smart pricing strategies, managing cash flow, and securing the right funding, you can build a strong financial foundation. Utilize available tools and resources, and don't hesitate to seek professional help when needed. With careful planning and diligent management, you'll be well-equipped to navigate the financial challenges of your business journey and achieve long-term success.

Case Studies/Examples

Case Study 1: The Rise of Eco-Goods Mart

Background

Eco-Goods Mart started as a small home-based business in 2018, focusing on eco-friendly products. The founder, Sarah, was passionate about sustainability and saw a growing demand for green products. She began by sourcing bamboo toothbrushes and reusable bags from local suppliers and selling them online.

Challenges

Sarah faced several challenges in the beginning:

- Limited capital for inventory.
- Difficulty finding reliable suppliers.
- Lack of online marketing experience.

Strategies

Sarah adopted the following strategies to overcome these challenges:

1. **Bootstrap Funding**: She started small, reinvesting her profits back into the business to gradually increase her inventory.
2. **Supplier Relationships**: She built strong relationships with a few key suppliers, ensuring quality and reliability.

3. **Digital Marketing**: She took online courses to learn about social media marketing and SEO, using platforms like Instagram and Facebook to reach her target audience.

Results

Within two years, Eco-Goods Mart expanded its product line to include eco-friendly household items, cosmetics, and apparel. Sales grew steadily, and Sarah opened her first physical store in 2020. The business now generates over $500,000 in annual revenue.

Case Study 2: TechZone's Wholesale Success

Background

TechZone started as a small wholesale distributor of electronics in 2016. The founder, Mark, had previous experience in the electronics industry and identified a niche in providing affordable, high-quality gadgets to small retailers.

Challenges

Mark encountered several obstacles:

- High competition in the electronics market.
- Maintaining a steady supply of high-demand products.
- Managing logistics and warehousing.

Strategies

Mark implemented the following strategies:

1. **Market Research**: He conducted thorough market research to identify high-demand products and potential gaps in the market.
2. **Supplier Diversification**: He sourced products from multiple suppliers to ensure a steady inventory and negotiated better terms.
3. **Efficient Logistics**: He invested in an efficient inventory management system and partnered with reliable logistics companies to streamline operations.

Results

TechZone's sales doubled each year for the first three years. Mark expanded his warehouse space and hired a dedicated sales team. By 2021, TechZone had established itself as a leading wholesale distributor, with a strong reputation for reliability and customer service.

Case Study 3: Boutique Bliss Goes Online

Background

Boutique Bliss was a small brick-and-mortar fashion boutique in a suburban area. The owner, Emily, faced declining foot traffic and increasing rent costs. In 2019, she decided to take her business online to reach a wider audience.

Challenges

Emily faced several hurdles:

- Transitioning from physical to online sales.
- Building an e-commerce website.
- Competing with larger online retailers.

Strategies

Emily used the following strategies to transition successfully:

1. **Website Development**: She invested in a professional e-commerce website with user-friendly navigation and a secure payment system.
2. **Social Media Engagement**: She leveraged social media platforms to showcase her products, engage with customers, and drive traffic to her website.

3. **Personalized Service**: She maintained the boutique's personalized service by offering virtual styling sessions and responsive customer support.

Results

Within a year, Boutique Bliss's online sales surpassed its previous in-store sales. Emily continued to grow her online presence, adding new product lines and collaborating with influencers. The business is now thriving, with a loyal customer base and strong online sales.

Case Study 4: Gourmet Delights Wholesale Expansion

Background

Gourmet Delights started as a small family-run gourmet food store in 2015. The owners, Alex and Maria, saw an opportunity to expand into wholesale by supplying specialty foods to local restaurants and cafes.

Challenges

They faced several challenges:

- Scaling up production to meet wholesale demand.
- Ensuring product quality and consistency.
- Navigating the regulatory requirements for food distribution.

Strategies

Alex and Maria adopted these strategies:

1. **Quality Control**: They implemented strict quality control measures to maintain the high standards of their products.
2. **Regulatory Compliance**: They invested in understanding and complying with all necessary food safety regulations.
3. **Market Penetration**: They used direct sales strategies, attending trade shows, and networking with local restaurant owners to secure wholesale contracts.

Results

Gourmet Delights quickly established a reputation for quality and reliability. Within three years, their wholesale division accounted for 60% of their total revenue. They now supply gourmet foods to over 50 restaurants and cafes and are exploring opportunities to expand regionally.

Case Study 5: Fitness Hub's Niche Market Strategy

Background

Fitness Hub began as a small online store specializing in fitness equipment and apparel in 2017. The founder, Jason, identified a niche market in high-quality, durable fitness gear for home workouts.

Challenges

Jason faced challenges such as:

- Limited initial customer base.
- High competition from established brands.
- Managing inventory and shipping logistics.

Strategies

Jason implemented the following strategies:

1. **Niche Focus**: He focused on a niche market, offering unique and high-quality products that were not widely available.
2. **Customer Reviews**: He encouraged satisfied customers to leave positive reviews and testimonials, building trust and credibility.
3. **Partnerships**: He partnered with fitness influencers and trainers to promote his products and reach a broader audience.

Results

Fitness Hub grew rapidly, with sales increasing by 150% year over year. By 2020, Jason had expanded his product line and built a loyal customer base. The business continues to thrive, with strong online sales and a growing community of fitness enthusiasts.

Case Study 6: Artisan Craft Collective's Community Focus

Background

Artisan Craft Collective started as a small online marketplace for handmade crafts in 2018. The founder, Lily, aimed to support local artisans by providing them with a platform to sell their creations.

Challenges

Lily encountered several challenges:

- Building a marketplace from scratch.
- Attracting both artisans and buyers to the platform.
- Managing the logistics of multiple sellers.

Strategies

Lily used the following strategies:

1. **Community Building**: She focused on building a strong community of artisans, providing support and resources to help them succeed.
2. **Marketing Campaigns**: She ran targeted marketing campaigns to attract buyers interested in unique, handmade products.
3. **Logistics Management**: She developed an efficient logistics system to handle the complexities of a multi-seller marketplace.

Results

Artisan Craft Collective quickly gained traction, with a growing number of artisans joining the platform. Within two years, the marketplace had over 200 active sellers and a loyal customer base. Lily's focus on community and quality helped establish the brand as a trusted source for handmade crafts.

Case Study 7: Pet Paradise's Customer-Centric Approach

Background

Pet Paradise started as a local pet supply store in 2016. The owner, Karen, was passionate about providing high-quality products and exceptional service to pet owners. She decided to expand her business by adding an online store and wholesale division.

Challenges

Karen faced challenges such as:

- Balancing in-store and online operations.
- Competing with large pet supply chains.
- Managing customer expectations and service.

Strategies

Karen adopted the following strategies:

1. **Customer Service Excellence**: She focused on providing exceptional customer service, both in-store and online, building a loyal customer base.
2. **Product Quality**: She ensured that all products met high-quality standards, sourcing from reputable suppliers.

3. **Marketing and Promotions**: She used targeted marketing and promotional campaigns to attract new customers and retain existing ones.

Results

Pet Paradise's online sales grew rapidly, complementing the in-store revenue. The wholesale division also took off, supplying products to other small pet stores. Karen's commitment to quality and service helped the business thrive, with a strong reputation in the local community and beyond.

Case Study 8: Trendy Threads' Social Media Success

Background

Trendy Threads started as a small online fashion boutique in 2018, targeting young adults with trendy and affordable clothing. The founder, Rachel, used her fashion sense and social media skills to build the brand.

Challenges

Rachel faced several challenges:

- Standing out in a crowded online fashion market.
- Building brand awareness and customer loyalty.
- Managing inventory and fast-changing fashion trends.

Strategies

Rachel implemented these strategies:

1. **Social Media Marketing**: She leveraged social media platforms like Instagram and TikTok to showcase her products and engage with customers.
2. **Influencer Collaborations**: She collaborated with fashion influencers to promote her brand and reach a wider audience.
3. **Responsive Inventory Management**: She used data analytics to track trends and adjust inventory accordingly.

Results

Trendy Threads quickly gained a large following on social media, driving significant traffic to the website. Sales grew steadily, and Rachel expanded her product line to include accessories and footwear. The business is now a popular online destination for fashion-conscious young adults.

Case Study 9: Green Grocers' Sustainable Growth

Background

Green Grocers began as a small organic grocery store in 2017. The founders, Tom and Lisa, were passionate about promoting healthy eating and sustainable practices. They decided to expand their business by adding a delivery service and a wholesale division for local restaurants.

Challenges

Tom and Lisa faced several challenges:

- Managing the logistics of perishable goods.
- Competing with larger grocery chains.
- Ensuring product quality and sustainability.

Strategies

They adopted the following strategies:

1. **Local Sourcing**: They sourced products from local farmers and producers, ensuring freshness and supporting the local economy.

- **Conclusion**

Chapter 1: Reflecting on Your Journey

As you reach the end of this guide, it's essential to take a moment to reflect on the journey you've embarked upon. Starting a wholesale and retail business is a significant endeavor that requires dedication, perseverance, and adaptability. You've learned about planning, sourcing, marketing, and managing your finances. Each step has been a crucial part of building a solid foundation for your business. Remember, every challenge you face is an opportunity to learn and grow.

Chapter 2: Key Takeaways

1. **Planning is Paramount**: Your business plan is your roadmap. It helps you stay focused and provides a clear path to follow.

2. **Source Smart**: Finding reliable suppliers and building strong relationships with them is vital for a seamless operation.

3. **Marketing Matters**: Effective marketing strategies are essential for attracting and retaining customers. Utilize both traditional and digital marketing methods to reach a wider audience.

4. **Financial Management**: Keeping your finances in check ensures your business stays afloat and profitable. Regularly review your financial statements and adjust your strategies accordingly.

Chapter 3: Embracing Continuous Learning

The business world is constantly evolving. New technologies, market trends, and consumer behaviors can significantly impact your business. Stay curious and open to learning. Attend industry conferences, join relevant forums, and continually educate yourself through books, courses, and seminars. Adaptability and willingness to innovate are key traits of successful entrepreneurs.

Chapter 4: Building a Community

Don't underestimate the power of networking. Building a community around your business can provide support, inspiration, and new opportunities. Connect with other business owners, join local business groups, and engage with your customers. A strong network can offer valuable insights and help you navigate challenges more effectively.

Chapter 5: Looking Ahead

Your journey doesn't end here. In fact, this is just the beginning. As you continue to grow your wholesale and retail business, set new goals and challenges for yourself. Celebrate your successes, no matter how small, and learn from your mistakes. Stay committed to your vision and keep pushing forward.

By following the guidance provided in this eBook and remaining dedicated to your business, you are well on your way to creating a successful and thriving wholesale and retail enterprise. The retail revolution starts with you. Embrace the journey, stay passionate, and watch your business flourish.

About the Author

Arya Gupta is an ambitious young entrepreneur who has recently embarked on the exciting journey of higher education, currently pursuing a B.Tech degree with a focus on Artificial Intelligence and Data Science at Arya College of Engineering and IT in Jaipur. At just 18 years old, Arya has already demonstrated remarkable entrepreneurial spirit by starting an online wholesale and retail business.

Passionate about both technology and commerce, Arya blends modern digital tools with innovative business strategies to navigate the competitive landscape of wholesale and retail. Despite the challenges of balancing college life and running a business, Arya remains dedicated to learning, growing, and achieving success.

In "Retail Revolution: The Ultimate Guide to Starting Your Wholesale and Retail Business," Arya shares practical insights and strategies gleaned from personal experience, aiming to inspire and guide fellow aspiring entrepreneurs on their path to business success.

Outside of academics and business, Arya enjoys dancing, acting, singing, and is also a fitness enthusiast. These activities provide a refreshing balance to a busy life. Arya is committed to continuous learning and looks forward to making a significant impact in both the business and tech worlds.

This book is a testament to Arya's belief that with determination, creativity, and the right guidance, anyone can turn their entrepreneurial dreams into reality.

Call to Action

Congratulations on completing "Retail Revolution: The Ultimate Guide to Starting Your Wholesale and Retail Business"! You now have the knowledge and tools to embark on your entrepreneurial journey with confidence and clarity.

But remember, knowledge is most powerful when put into action. Here are a few steps you can take right now to start making your business dreams a reality:

1. **Define Your Vision:**
    - Take some time to outline your business goals and vision. What kind of wholesale or retail business do you want to create? What are your short-term and long-term objectives?
2. **Conduct Market Research:**
    - Use the strategies outlined in this book to research your target market, identify potential customers, and understand your competition. This will help you make informed decisions and refine your business plan.
3. **Create a Business Plan:**
    - Develop a detailed business plan that includes your business model, marketing strategies, financial projections, and operational plans. A solid business plan is essential for securing funding and guiding your business.
4. **Start Small:**
    - Begin with a manageable scope to test your ideas and learn from your experiences. This will allow you to make adjustments and scale your business gradually.

5. **Network and Seek Mentorship:**
    - Connect with other entrepreneurs, join relevant industry groups, and seek mentorship from experienced business owners. Learning from others can provide valuable insights and support.
6. **Stay Persistent and Adaptable:**
    - Entrepreneurship is a journey filled with challenges and opportunities. Stay persistent, be open to learning, and adapt to changes in the market. Your resilience will be a key factor in your success.
7. **Stay Connected:**
    - I would love to hear about your progress and experiences! Feel free to connect with me on social media or through my website. Share your journey, ask questions, and stay updated with additional resources and insights.
    - iaryaguptaa@gmail.com
    - INSTAGRAM: @i_aryaguptaa

Don't forget to visit my E-commerce website too~

LINK: https://manabhavanindustries.com/

8. **Leave a Review:**
    - If you found this book helpful, please consider leaving a review on the Platforms where you purchased this E- Book. Your feedback helps other readers discover this resource and supports my work.

Thank you for choosing "Retail Revolution" as your guide. Your entrepreneurial journey is just beginning, and I am excited to see where it takes you. Remember, every great business starts with a single step – take that step today!

www.ingramcontent.com/pod-product-compliance
Lightning Source LLC
Chambersburg PA
CBHW082239220526
45479CB00005B/1278